Was close to love

It wasn't just close, it was very close.

By - Shivam Antapuriya

How was it when I was close to love? even if it was there, why was it there? Even if it was our fault then why was it? Even if a mistake is made It was not just one person's fault If it was only one then that one Why are you not alone even after being alone?

1-

When I met you, I did not just meet you, but I also found peace, comfort, passion and much more in my empty bag.

You are searching for me and I am searching for you, maybe this search will also remain a search in this life.

when you touch my hair, I was very angry I used
to get angry even when you questioned my hair.
But till date I have not been able to show you
that anger whenever I remember that past. then
I get angry again Why could I never say anything
Why couldn't I be angry at you? Probably all
questions will remain unanswered

I do not only remember your hug, I still remember your questioning while looking into my eyes.

What is love?

Love is not something that can be done only with
a girl. Sometimes sitting with your friends and
laughing and joking,

Talking about your heart, talking about breakups, patch-ups, telling your friends everything that you cannot tell your family members.

You may not be able to call it love, but...?

All these feelings take you very close to love and teach you love...

You are sitting alone or going back in the past, you start feeling what used to be a bygone moment of yours and theirs.

I can end everything, if only that one photo of yours was not there, looking at which till date I dream with open eyes.

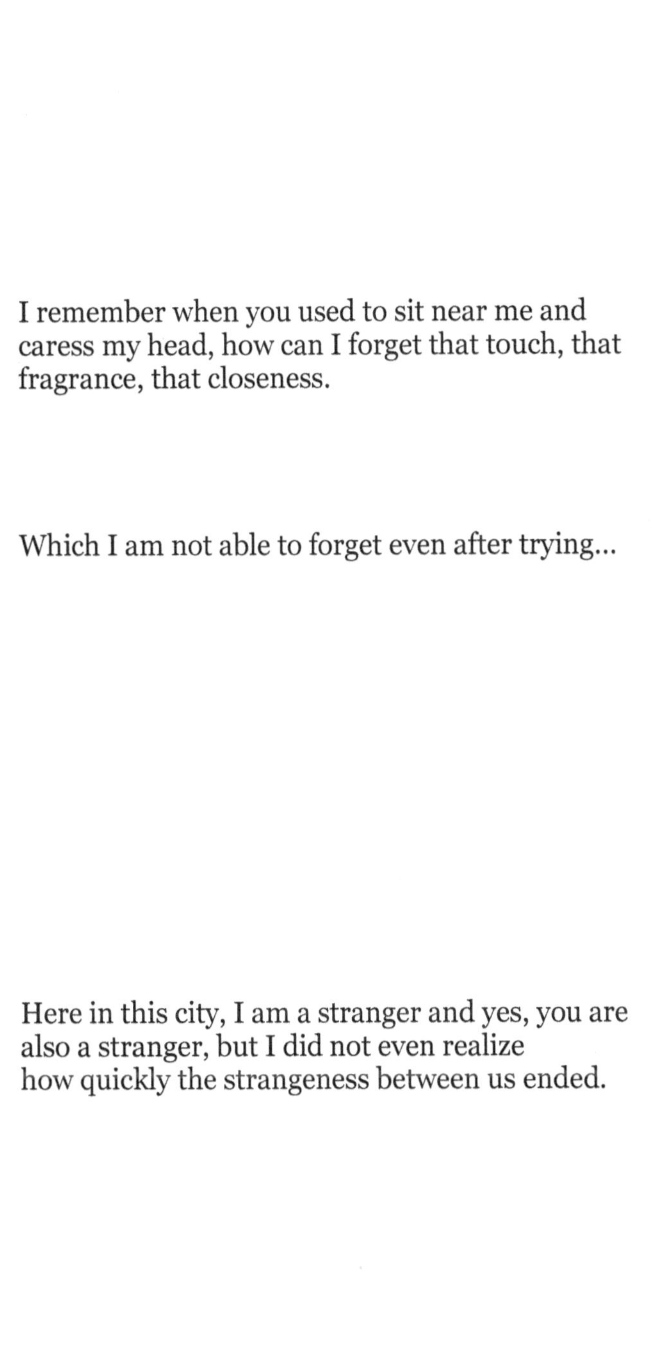

I remember when you used to sit near me and
caress my head, how can I forget that touch, that
fragrance, that closeness.

Which I am not able to forget even after trying...

Here in this city, I am a stranger and yes, you are
also a stranger, but I did not even realize
how quickly the strangeness between us ended.

When did I get into your lake-like deep eyes,
perhaps I did not know and neither did you...

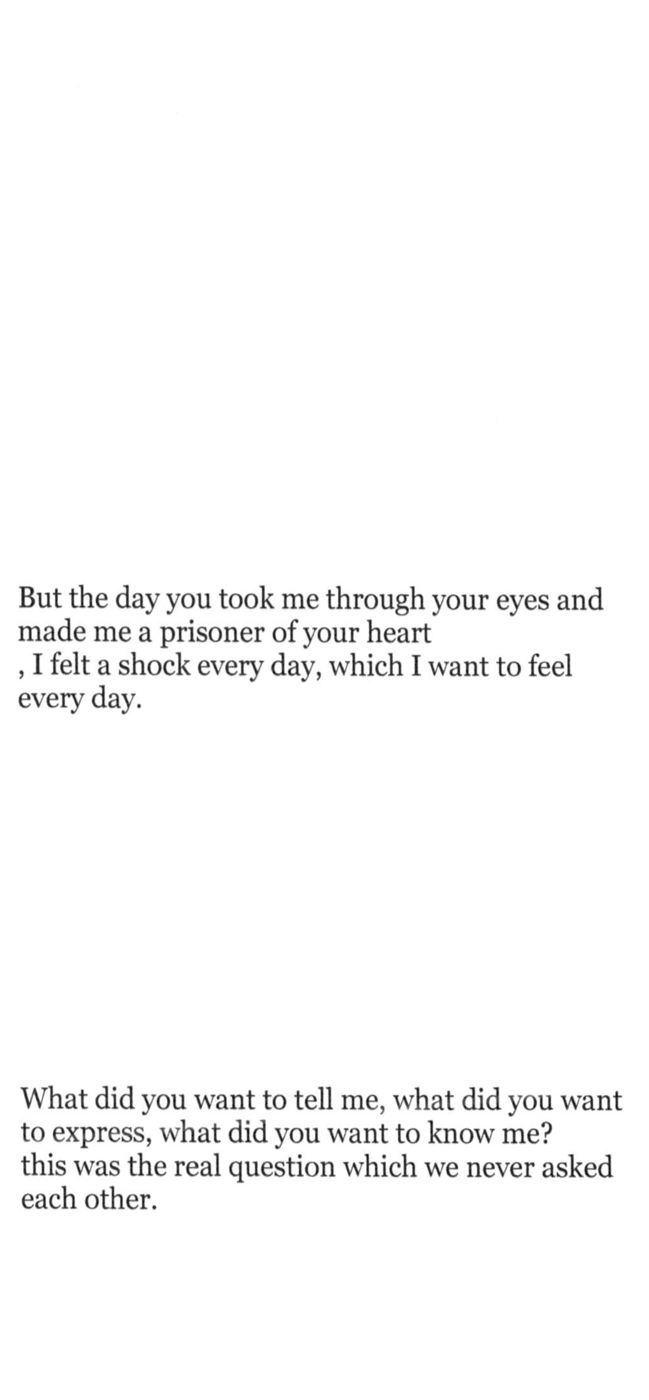

But the day you took me through your eyes and
made me a prisoner of your heart
, I felt a shock every day, which I want to feel
every day.

What did you want to tell me, what did you want
to express, what did you want to know me?
this was the real question which we never asked
each other.

Where words could not work between us, then gestures were useful... What will you call this......?

Whether you were mine or not, whether I will be yours or not, this will also remain a question.

Whereas in love, every question is not a question mark but a sign of love.

What all did you not want to know, what all did I not want to tell, your eyes expressed even more than this without saying anything. Your eyes...

You wanted to keep me with you like a perfume,
that would make you smell good for some time...

But I wanted to become your clothes and stay
with you the whole day...

When you wanted to make me your clothes and
keep me with you
, then I wanted to become the beauty of your face
and stay with you for the whole life...

This was everything between us, which was different from everyone else
, which made you and me completely different from all these people of the society...

Holding me in your arms, getting lost in your arms,

my heart still feels the same. Before boarding the train, you pulled me towards you in one go.

The strange sensation that had taken place in my
heart at that moment and the strange

heartbeats that had arisen in my heart for that
sensation,

I want to feel those heartbeats continuously in
myself every day.

You had not only snatched my used tea cup from
me, to tell you the truth,

today I understood that you had snatched not
only that cup of tea but probably all my rights.

When you had put my used tea cup to your
lips......

Maybe that cup had stopped while saying
something to me...

What did my cup want to say, I could not ask it, I
will regret this until that time comes back again
yet again...?

And yes, when your used tea cup came in my hands,

it had just looked at me with a slight smile in its eyes, the meaning of which you all must be knowing...?

When the used tea cups were being exchanged,
the night had come to a standstill.
The time taken in seconds felt as if many years
had passed in those very seconds...

Love is also that in which...

Some under a tree, some at a tea stall, some at a college library seat, staring at the empty seat in the class without informing each other. If this was not love, then what was it?

The result was that one was sobbing here and the other there...

Your killing me without reason and my killing
you,
without reason was saying something which both
of them were not able to name till now.

If they thought it was wrong to give perfume and handkerchief, then what was the problem in accepting the rose?

A friend is crying after getting perfume as a gift from his girlfriend, whereas I am the same even after getting a handkerchief...

The first meeting when he was sitting on the sea,
t next to us and kept smiling and perhaps was
saying something through his eyes,
we were unable to understand what he was
trying to say,
and should we understand him, what was he
trying to explain to me.

What a strange story it is that two strangers meet
for a few moments and become each other's for
all the moments of their life.

Later he himself told me that I was feeling
irritated with you that day without meeting,
without recognizing, without speaking, why is
this so...?

When someone has left home after getting ready
for the first meeting with his lover,
then he remembers his past,
whose pain is still a tenant of his heart, then
what must he be going through.

2-

Perhaps this pain may be of any one of you
This love is no less than a pain which you want to
lose and you don't want to lose it either.
When it is lost, we start looking for it and when
that pain settles inside us, we want to keep it
away from ourselves.

But...
But by then it is too late.

I got the sign of her love when her eyes looked at
my eyes to their heart's content and it was like a
soft kiss of the eyes.

Today, these eyes had tasted this soft kiss which
perhaps they did not want to forget.
They wanted me to get this taste every day, to
stay with me, to stay with me as long as we are
alive.

On that very day, I got the message of my love
, whose path perhaps... perhaps... perhaps... was
those heart touching waves.

Heart touching waves are those waves whose contact cannot be cut off normally until those waves themselves disappear.

Have you ever loved, has anyone ever loved you, have you ever felt what love is like...

Perhaps this question of love will remain a
question in itself

If yes, then keep doing it, do it as much as you
can, but "if no, then don't do it" I will not say
this, try it, even if you start with an object, do it
with your heart, do it with your father, do it with
your family,
Do it with someone or the other,
when you don't find anyone worth loving
anywhere
, then listen to us once and try loving yourself.

When you don't find anyone worth loving in this
world, then don't go anywhere,
just try to see yourself in such a way that you
start seeing something like love in yourself and
try, you will fall in love with yourself in just one
attempt,

try it...

I don't know if someone loves you or not, but I am close to you, I have heard that being close makes one fall in love,

maybe I will succeed...

When you call, you talk without any reason.
I know that you know the answers but still you
ask me the same question again and again.

My heart is far away from you but you bring it close to me through your talks because I know that you love me.

I have still treasured the rose you gave me on Valentine's Day. I don't know why you gave it to me but I don't feel like throwing it away.

I can still see each of its dry and broken petals
when I open the book in which it is kept.
That rose given by you.

I have kept that rose only as a memory of you
and not in your love.

Still, maybe you don't know that I am close to
love but I am not dissolved in love.

When you sit near me then that touch, that
wrinkle, that cold wave brings the water of the
ocean and fills my heart.

Whose waves we are unable to handle, which we
dedicate to you by giving them the form of love.

Whenever our hearts meet and you go far away
from us, then a voice comes from the heart,
that your union is like the sea meeting the sky at
the ports.

Getting wet together in the rain Do you
remember? When I refused, you used to pour
water on me.
I had no desire to get wet in the rain and you
used to forcefully drag me into the raining
clouds. Do you remember when you were very
scared when there was a thunderbolt?
When you screamed and held me in your arms

I know you go to the temple, mosque,
Gurudwara and sit there, write her name, waste
hours of time to see her,
just to hear her tell me by looking into my eyes,
that you don't love me.
I know a voice resonates inside you which forces
your ears to tell you that she is there and you go
and meet her there,
whether you have come to study, or to have tea,
or to take a walk. What is this, are you not able to
understand yourself ?

Yes, this is what happens when someone is close
to love.....
If she comes to the class wearing clothes of the
same color as you are wearing,
then your heart starts beating fast, doesn't it?
And you secretly look at each other, a line of
embarrassment is drawn between you.
Then is this where what we want to say starts.

When someone has called you to meet, the time
has been fixed and you are late,
what all does not happen inside you,

Then when he is seen coming in front of us, then
we return to the old courtyard....

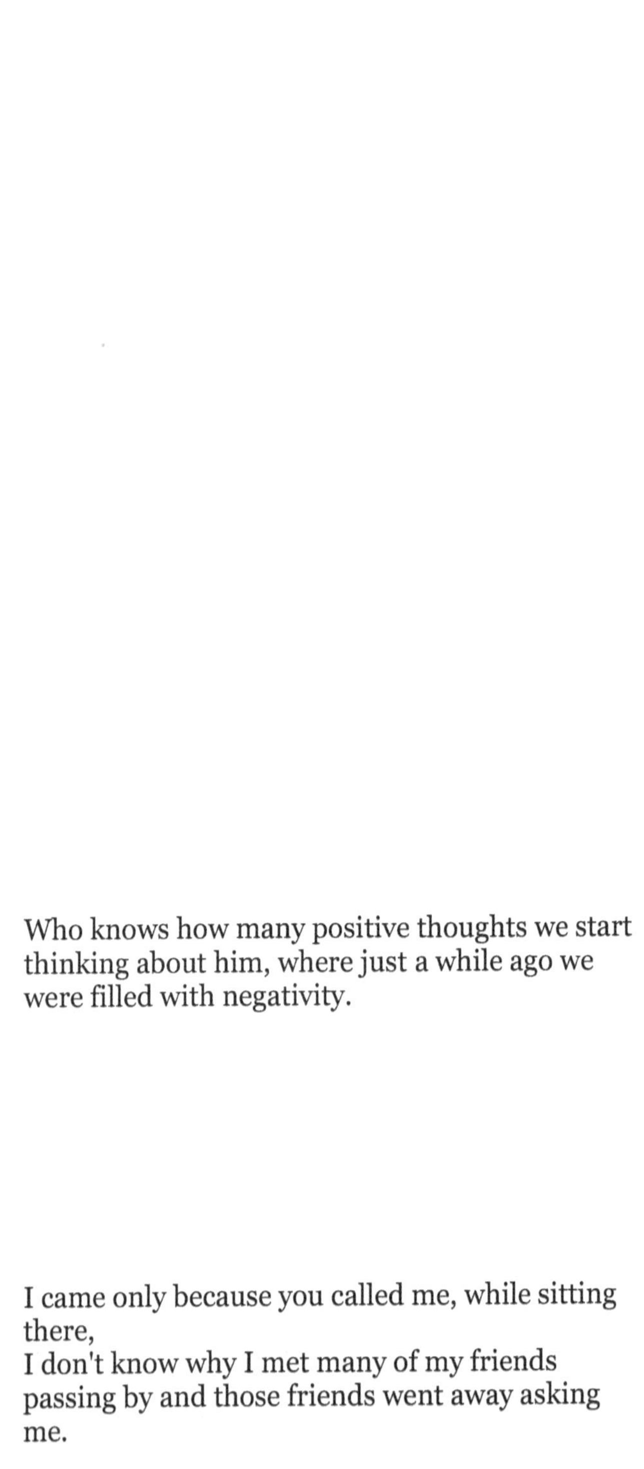

Who knows how many positive thoughts we start
thinking about him, where just a while ago we
were filled with negativity.

I came only because you called me, while sitting
there,
I don't know why I met many of my friends
passing by and those friends went away asking
me.

so many questions in that short time,
the answers to which I did not have then and
now, maybe I will never be able to give those
answers.

When he asked me repeatedly,
I could not mention you, I did not have the
courage to tell him why I am here,
I just smiled and said that I have come just like
that.

3-

While that smile was telling everything,
my speaking in a hurry and looking here and
there to make sure that you don't come at this
time, otherwise I will not be able to hide the lie
which I am telling to hide the truth.

Today he came again on your call, till now he had finished five chocolates, one biscuit and one coconut water and had received phone calls from two- three of his friends,

But you neither came nor received a single phone
call.

Many old university friends with whom he had
talked on chat,
when the chat ended, to pass time he was
reading the chat of those friends alone,
he was reading messages from both sides, he was
alone.

He had a lot of anger in his heart for you, but he was not able to express it. As soon as you came, everything changed. The whole atmosphere which was very calm, was filled with the chirping of birds.

Till now the shade of the tree was giving me peace and coolness from the heat of my anger, suddenly I don't know why I started feeling jealous of that.

I was thinking why these birds, who could have
dispelled my loneliness, have not chirped yet

Now that I am not alone, why are they also
talking to me,
Why are they starting to make their voices heard,
do they have any complaints with us.

The first time you were in the room with me
, I was getting a kind of peace which we always
want to feel.

You did not seem like you to me
, you were not at all what you were from the
inside,

When you came and sat with me, a kind of
alienation had come inside me.

You had suddenly placed your head on my
shoulder holding my armpit, I have carried that
inner fragrance within me till today.

Then the first time you touched my forehead with your lips while hugging me can never be recalled from my memory lines.

I feel like you keep hitting me and I just keep looking at you.

I don't know why I want to know how hard you
can hit me and how much pain I can feel.
I don't think those soft hands of yours will hurt
me.

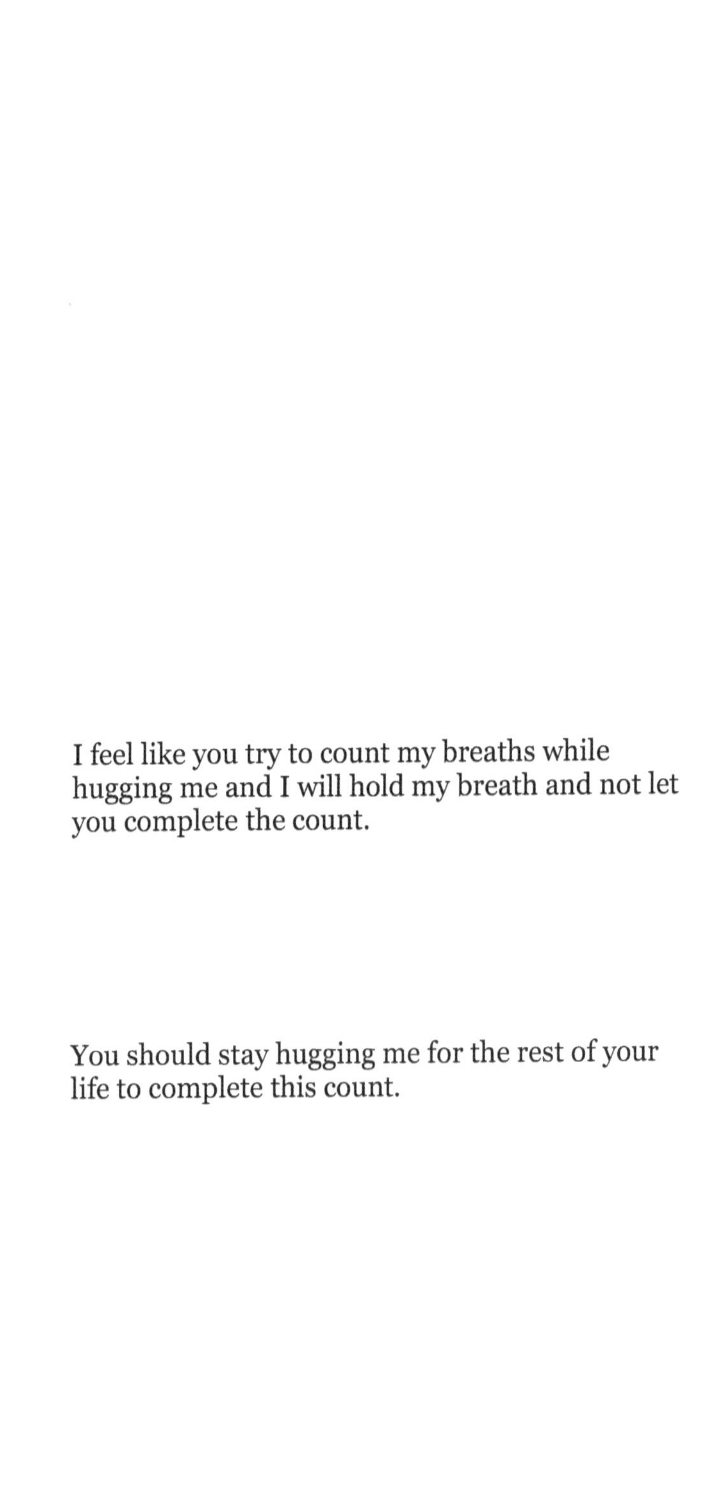

I feel like you try to count my breaths while
hugging me and I will hold my breath and not let
you complete the count.

You should stay hugging me for the rest of your
life to complete this count.

I definitely go to drink tea alone but when I meet you, the taste of tea itself changes the style of every sip.

Because with every sip, the taste of one or the
other thing you said also gets into the tea.

Maybe you will keep trying forever but still we
will not be able to find you… And yes, maybe we
will also leave this earth trying to find you…

But you to us and we to you, maybe and maybe
and maybe...

I know this incident must have happened to you
too when someone close to you would have asked
you who are you...?

Who are you to interfere in my life...

Like I had told someone a few years ago that
what is my past is nothing more now...

I have changed so much for someone else that
my morning used to start with a cup of tea in one
hand and newspaper on the table.

Today the same morning has started with a
phone in hand to see your good morning
message.

Do you remember, you yourself had said, that
you and you, I don't think you will be able to
change even a bit and that too for someone else.

Today I myself am unable to understand why and for whom we are changing ourselves, for those who were never mine or will never be mine , maybe for them...

If all this is true then why am I doing this...?

Your morning Whatsapp (WP) messages, the drizzling drops of rain, your attitude on top of it. All these together have changed my morning completely and you, you don't even look around it.

Do you remember when I questioned your love, you answered from your mind that I am the same as I was before...

You don't need to think too much,
if you have any priority then it is me, if we have
any priority then it is you...

It is not so easy to say all this to someone as
easily as he said it to me,
he himself had asked the question and he had
also given the answer to that question which we
should have given.

Now if this is not close to love then what else
would you call it...?

We were both on the same bed, he was talking to himself and I was working on my laptop and listening to a ghazal by Jagjit ji, Yeh Daulat Bhi Le Lo Yeh Shohrat Bhi Le Lo...

You used to say that I want to be with such a person with whom I can feel completely safe even if I am alone, which you probably saw in me today.

Every time I met you, it felt like I was meeting a new person again.

There was so much newness in you, so much openness in you, I kept seeing this only with my closed and open eyes

That day, running, shouting, you held me in your arms, I was scared but you were feeling very safe, right?

You had told me that you had done all this
without any reason,
you were also giving some signals which you
understood and I kept ignoring.

I felt like I had become a small poem for you and
you were like a story in a novel for me, changing
characters at every step.

Whenever you were in our room,
a strange smell would emanate from my room,
which I have not been able to find out till date,
where that smell came from and where it went,
even though I was still close to that smell like
you.

4 –

When tears used to drip from your lake-like deep
eyes and end their life trying to roll down from
the desert of your cheeks,
I used to pity those tears more than you because
they were innocent in not reaching their
destination.

Because I wanted those tears to complete their
life in my handkerchief....

I still remember you talking to me Because your
style of talking is different What is it that when
you talk
An aura is created All around me
I get covered by its cover.

What is called getting absorbed

Something similar happens when I meet you

Even without meeting you I feel that you are with
me

It is not your voice but it feels that you are in
front of me in person.

This love also works like a sink in which all the water comes back down no matter where you pour it.

You may be in love with some other body part or beauty but it gets stuck in the heart only...

He wanted to sprinkle my love on himself like perfume. He wanted to shine by applying a thin layer of my love.
He wanted to get the heat and brightness of the sun with my love. It was this love with which he wanted to snatch me from himself, which he might be trying to do perhaps, yes perhaps even today.

Why do you forget that I am spending very
important moments of my busy life on you but I
don't know if you will try to understand it or if
you do.

I always feel very lonely even when I am with
you.

Which I cannot express to anyone, even if I do, to
whom because I don't have anyone of my own...

Do you think I will lose life or lose to myself, yes
maybe I will lose to myself but still I will win
over you....

Do you remember that deserted alley of a
deserted city when you kept walking holding my
hands tightly in yours.....

I wanted to get away from you,

I was wondering how soon you would free me
from your arms, But my heart didn't feel like
getting away from you.

What was that fear of love or love with fear!
Maybe yes love...

I have kept the fragrance of your hair imprisoned
in that room till now, 2 whole years have passed,
I have not opened that room, only because of the
fear that the wind might blow away that lovely
fragrance and take it with itself.

I still remember, maybe you remember that day when we both sat on the railway track in the evening and went....

Both of us ate from the same Paan, it was your insistence that we both should eat from the same Paan.

Do you remember those winter days when you brought a burger for me in Nuvis, how the light of the moon shining in the sky was coming closer to our shadows.

What difference does it make now, those
memories have remained just memories,

When did that evening turn into night,

For me, only one word comes out of your mind,
how strange you are

I don't hide anything, yet some of my own people
tell me, friend, you are a very hidden warrior.

I used to say, what difference does it make, but
now I understand that it does matter,
only that one should understand who belongs to
whom and how much.

Do you remember, when I was with you in your city, in the auto, you held me tight in your arms in such a way, as if I would get lost somewhere, then I understood how scared you are of losing me.

I know, when I was sick, you were with you, you
spent the whole night changing the bandages on
our foreheads.
I know, you knew more about my body every
moment than I did.

You had caressed every corner of my body, You
had lost your sleep for me, And you had made
my pain your own.

In the morning, when I got some rest,
I was looking at his eyes which were awake the
whole night and he was searching for love in my
eyes.

Then I started thinking how after sacrificing his
sleep the whole night and doing everything for
me, he didn't say a single word and after saying
to me very lovingly (take care of yourself) he
went to the university to give a lecture.

I didn't stop you from going,
Because you don't get the one you love the most,

Maybe if I would have stopped you for me, you
would have gone,

But I didn't stop you, even then you couldn't go,
Because you must be feeling that we are close to
love, maybe...

Then my love is not this, your love is what you
are not saying.

You were leaving me and going, I didn't stop you,
but I didn't even agree that you didn't go.

Then why didn't you go, there was something
that stopped you, I remember how many times
you have sat outside a cafe holding my palm in
yours, I remember how many times you have
walked around that shop holding a cup of tea.

I did not force you to go,
Because I knew you would not be able to go, you
would not be able to erase my memories, the
peace you get with me will hardly be found
anywhere else.

Maybe I have started liking you even without
seeing you

I have started liking your voice even without
hearing you

I have started talking to you without saying
anything.

Those few incidents which start from the eyes of the hero and heroine and build a palace on the land of the heart.

The palace becomes so big that even the beds of both of them get decorated in it.

Those incidents have not started from your eyes
but from your words, that too without hearing
those words, this incident has happened...

I get worried thinking what will happen when
our eyes will meet, then maybe a big incident will
happen which may have never happened before.

5 –

I don't know how good you feel when you are
with me,
but when I am alone, every moment feels
burdensome to me.

I remember that winter evening when we went
out for a drive,

It was bitterly cold, it was your insistence that we
go for a drive,
the chill that could not get out of the car was
welcoming me with open arms.

You were sitting in the back seat, staring at me, I
don't know why and what.

I opened one of the windows on your side and
soon closed it, and you quickly left the back seat
and came and sat on the seat next to the driving
seat,
Then you crossed your hands and hugged me
and said, Oh! Yaar, it is so cold.

I just smiled in response.

In a short while, both your hands became like a garland around my left hand and you were trying to rest on my shoulder.

After driving for a few more minutes, I stopped
the car in front of that hotel whose methi paratha
was on everyone's lips in those days.

I didn't want to disturb your sleep, but for those
fifteen to twenty minutes, I kept caressing your
forehead and hair while sitting in the car.

Due to the heat inside the car, a crust had formed on your pink lips, due to which your lips looked withered.

To remove that crust, I gave you a long, unbroken kiss, due to which your lips became pink again and bloomed like rose buds.

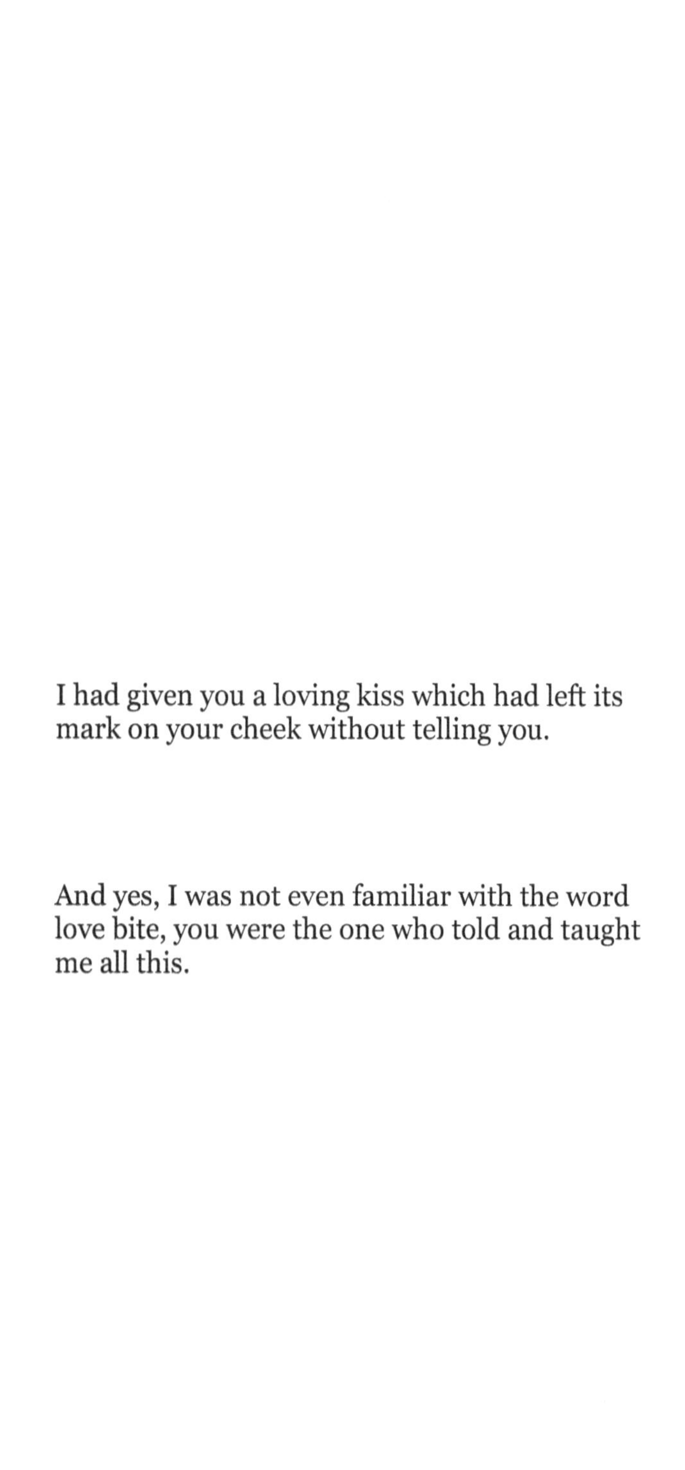

I had given you a loving kiss which had left its mark on your cheek without telling you.

And yes, I was not even familiar with the word love bite, you were the one who told and taught me all this.

You were making sounds of oon m... oon m... oon m... without waking up when I was kissing you.

Then I kissed your forehead and you woke up and hugged me tightly and looked into my eyes as if you had said everything.

In a short while, there were pairs of fenugreek parathas and cups of clove cardamom tea in front of you as if saying that we both come together in the same plate but go separately in each other's hands.

Likewise, you both should also not stay together forever.

You were snatching parathas from my mouth
and eating them again and again and I was just
looking at your face, your childishness, your
carefreeness, your love and yes, seeing all this, I
went into your past and suddenly got lost in the
future.

It was not as easy for me to talk to you on chat all night as it was for you.

You talked to me from night till 5:00 PM in the morning, my reply was that I cannot do this...

When you proposed marriage to me in casual conversation,

I explained to you by taking the help of being the youngest in the house, try to understand me, I cannot do all this so soon, and especially to you....

The affection that is visible inside you, isn't it? where did you get that from How do you keep this innocence that is reflected in you with you? In the morning you become like the rising sun, in the evening you become like the setting sun. And at night you look no less than the moon

You are the eldest in your house and I am the youngest in my house, taking the help of this being the youngest, I explained to you, maybe you understood,

or you misunderstood me, I don't know...

~ Shivam Antapuriya